YOUR BOOK OF
TABLE TENNIS

The YOUR BOOK Series

YOUR BOOK OF
TABLE TENNIS

VICTOR BARNA

Drawings by
Alan Smith

FABER AND FABER
3 Queen Square
London

First published in 1971
by Faber and Faber Limited
3 Queen Square London WC1N 3AU
Reprinted 1974
Printed in Great Britain by
Latimer Trend & Company Ltd Plymouth

ISBN 0 571 09345 0

Contents

Illustrations

I

The Background to Modern Table Tennis

Although table tennis was played as far back as 1900, the International Table Tennis Federation, which governs the game, was not initiated until January 1926 following a discussion in Berlin between some of the pioneers of the game, including Dr. Lehmann of Germany, the Hon. Ivor Montagu of England, Zoltan Mechlovits of Hungary, Zdenek Heydusek of Czechoslovakia.

As a result, the first World Championship took place in London at the end of the same year and was attended by nine associations, representing Austria, Czechoslovakia, Denmark, England, Germany, Hungary, India, Sweden and Wales. The first congress of the newly formed I.T.T.F. took place at the same time; the Hon. Ivor Montagu was elected President and kept his position until 1967 when Roy Evans of Wales, who had been Secretary of the I.T.T.F. for nearly twenty years, succeeded him.

Until 1935, which brought the entry of the U.S.A., world table tennis was virtually European table tennis, as the Indian team which entered was selected from the Indian students residing in London. In 1937 Egypt joined the I.T.T.F. and two years later the organizing of the Championships went outside Europe for the first time, to Cairo. Only eleven Associations were able to make this longer than usual journey, and war broke out before it could be seen whether there might be a further extension of the game outside Europe.

9

In 1947 the first post-war World Championships were held in Paris, and shortly afterwards countries like Trinidad and Tobago and Palestine joined the International scene, later followed by countries from South America. In 1950 New Zealand took part for the first time and the following year the numbers were further increased by the arrival of Vietnam, Iran and Israel.

The big stepping-stone was reached in 1952 when the World Championships went again outside Europe, this time to Bombay. This naturally led to great awakening of interest in Asia, and the affiliation of the Associations of Japan, Cambodia, Pakistan, Hong Kong, Singapore, Afghanistan, Burma and the Republic of Korea came as a natural development.

Although in Bombay the men's singles was won by a Japanese, Satoh, Europeans still dominated the events; it was obvious that sooner or later the tremendous ability of the Japanese would have to be reckoned with, and it was not long—two years later—that with the peculiar penholder grip they swept all before them.

For the first time, China played, but was not very successful and did not enter the following year.

This was the time when the game underwent a far-reaching change. Introduced by the Japanese, sponge rubber bats revolutionized the technique of the game. Not only were some of the newcomers who used them almost impossible to beat, but old players who had seemed past their best suddenly found a new lease of life. The problem was that the sponge produced such unpredictable and unaccustomed strokes that not even those used to it could really control their game. There was a great controversy about the merits and demerits of the new 'weapon' and it was not until 1959 in Stockholm that the question was settled finally.

In the meantime, the Japanese continued along their triumphant road but the Chinese, using the same penholder grip as the Japanese, were not far behind them and showed considerable promise.

It might be worth mentioning that from 1937 until about the time of the arrival of the Japanese, defensive play had rather the better of the attacking players and the sport lost some of its spectacle, some games lasting for hours. One in particular went on for over eight hours and eventually it was not finished at all. This led to the lowering of the net from $6\frac{3}{4}$ in to 6 in.

Until 1957 the World Championships were held annually, but then because of the financial burdens on the organizing country and the participants, whose numbers increased year after year, it was decided to have the World Championships every two years instead of annually.

The rules and the type of game played have been the same for the last ten years and no changes are likely in the near future.

There are two further points worth mentioning which will show how interest in table tennis has grown ever wider:

(1) One of the most successful World Championships ever organized was that in Peking in 1961 when, in a stadium specially built for table tennis, 15,000 spectators watched the Tournament at every session with thousands waiting outside.
(2) The number of countries affiliated to the I.T.T.F. today numbers nearly a hundred.

2

Choice of Bat

Not so long ago the choice of bat was a very simple matter. The rules allowed a bat to be of any size, shape or form, therefore if you played with a frying-pan nobody could object; the rules simply could not stop anybody using it.

Nevertheless it was universally accepted that a bat made of plywood and covered with pimpled rubber sheeting was the best combination to play with. This happy state of affairs lasted until 1952 when, as I mentioned earlier, the Japanese came on the scene and brought with them a bat which consisted of plywood covered with sponge rubber of various thicknesses; the thicker the sponge the more difficult it was to control the ball. At times not only could the opponent not handle the oncoming ball, but the player using the new type of bat had no control over it either. Naturally, the game suffered through this new development and controversy raged for a number of years until the International Table Tennis Federation were able to agree to make a precise rule.

These are the types of bats which are now approved by the laws of the game:

(1) A bat made of wood and covered with standard pimpled

←Rubber not to exceed 2 mm.

Fig. 1 (a). Side elevation of rubber-covered bat

rubber sheeting provided that the thickness of the rubber does not exceed 2 mm on each side.

(2) A wooden bat covered with sponge and the sponge in turn covered with pimpled rubber sheeting with the pimples outside (generally called a Sandwich bat) and here again, the combined thickness of the sponge and rubber together must not exceed 4 mm on each side.

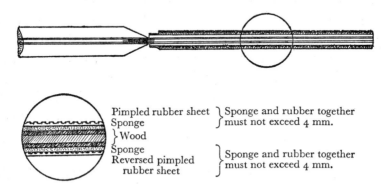

Pimpled rubber sheet } Sponge and rubber together
Sponge   } must not exceed 4 mm.
} Wood
Sponge
Reversed pimpled   } Sponge and rubber together
rubber sheet   } must not exceed 4 mm.

FIG. 1 (b). Side elevation of bat. Sponge and rubber

(3) As (2) except that the pimpled rubber is turned on the inside, giving a smooth playing surface (which is generally called the Soft or Back Side).

(4) Besides these three bats, any combination of the three can be used, that is, one can use the number (1) type on one side of the bat and another type on the other side providing that both sides are of the same colour.

(5) Bat made of wood, without any covering.

Although the rules state that the thickness of the rubber and sponge together must not exceed 4 mm, it does not mean that everybody wants the maximum thickness of the covering. Consequently, there are many players who use sponge of 1 mm, 1·5 mm up to 2 mm which again provides a varied range.

13

No need to tell you, therefore, that for a beginner or a youngster, it must be quite a problem deciding which bat to play with, and I must confess that this is a tricky problem, far more difficult than one would like to admit.

Before giving my opinion, let me say that there are two schools of thought. There are experts who say that it is better for the beginner to play straight away with the bat he is going to use later on, so they recommend the use of a Sandwich or Soft bat, which means that the bat plays a more important part than the body, footwork, ball control, etc. On the other hand, many coaches believe that it is better for a player to start with an ordinary pimpled rubber bat, which has not got the same speed as the other bats, and with which it is important for a player to put his body behind a stroke, use his feet and learn the game correctly. Naturally, both of these methods have their advantages and disadvantages.

Generally speaking, if I have to recommend a bat to a player whom I have not seen in action, I would suggest that someone with athletic qualities, speed and footwork—a person who is able to jump and run—should begin with the ordinary pimpled rubber bat and then change over when he finds that he can obtain more advantages from his Sandwich bat. In this way he will learn much of the rudiments of the game and the simple way of learning. On the other hand, people who may be slow on their feet but have very good natural reflexes, who prefer to stay at the table and play mostly a half-volley type of game, are probably better off starting straight away with the Sandwich bat.

As I have said before, it is difficult to say which method is the best one. I can only say that the Asians got the better of the Europeans because they were able to mix the old type of game with the new one, and that in spite of the fact that the majority of their players are using Sandwich bats, they still play with their bodies and their feet, getting the best out of both types of game.

There is just one more thing I would like to add. Do not throw away your bat and buy a new one just because you lose one game. Whatever you try, give it a good chance, and eventually you will come to the right conclusion. Also keep it in your mind that what is good for your club-mate who is a champion, may not necessarily be good for you as well. It is a very old habit to imitate better players, the proved champions, which is as it should be but please do not forget that people are not all alike—they differ in height, human qualities, etc.—and if you make a thorough study of champions, you will find that they themselves have different methods from one another. Just as in lawn tennis, Rod Laver plays a different game from Lew Hoad, so in table tennis does Ito, the Japanese world champion, play a different game from Ebbie Scholer of Germany, who was recently narrowly beaten in the 1969 world's final.

3

Starting to Play

Why is table tennis such a popular sport?

It is played in cold countries, England, Germany, Scandinavia, Central Europe, and in the hot climates of India, Africa and South America, and while in Europe it is generally looked on as a winter sport, in many parts of the world it is played all the year round, so climate itself has little bearing on its popularity.

I think it is popular because it appeals very much to young people. It is not expensive, the requisites are simple and the rules are not complicated. It can be started at an early age and a little success then will make you ambitious to do better.

When should you start to play? I have said that it can be started at an early age but this will depend on your height. If you are not tall enough to reach the balls, naturally you will begin to play with a very cramped style which later will be a handicap to you and difficult to change. I have seen children with a lot of talent doing very well at an early age, even winning Junior Championships, and then fading away because of their cramped style. When you have played this way for a number of years it will be difficult to change your style.

I will illustrate my point by telling the story of Ann-Haydon-Jones. Ann's father, Adrian Haydon, was one of England's great table tennis players, but Ann herself was not interested in sport, not even table tennis, and she would not go to see her father play. Then at the age of twelve she became very ill and the doctors told her that to overcome her illness she must play as much sport as possible. She therefore began to play table tennis, and later lawn tennis, and within a year or two she had become a table tennis champion of a very high standard.

I believe that if you start at the age of, say, ten, you will not reach a certain level until about thirteen or fourteen and I think that the same level could be reached if you started at twelve or thirteen.

I would like to emphasize, therefore, that the time to start to play table tennis will depend on your height and not your age. Perhaps, too, if you start to play at a very early age, by the time you are a teenager you may have lost some of your interest or enthusiasm, and today, of course, there are many other outlets for your energy—dancing, for instance, or any of the other sports.

I am sure that if you take up table tennis most of you will want to become champions and will do your best to improve your game, but remember that if you cannot become a champion, to improve your game will enable you to get so much more fun out of it.

I wish you every success and hope that the following chapters will help you to realize your ambitions.

4

The Grip

How should you hold a bat? Your choice is limited to two possibilities, nevertheless the decision can be a hard one. The East Asians, as I have said, have achieved considerable success in recent years by using mainly the so-called 'penholder' grip,

FIG. 2. Penholder grip

whilst for a long, long time it was agreed that the best method was the orthodox grip.

It is hardly necessary to explain what the difference is between the two, because the names themselves describe them. For the penholder grip the forefinger and the thumb go around the handle and the bat is held as you would hold a pen, the other three fingers lying on the other side of the bat.

18

The orthodox grip is sometimes called the 'handshake' grip, because this is the best way to describe it. Just shake hands with the bat, which must be well bedded into the hand; the blade itself, not the handle, should be held. The handle is used only to strengthen the grip.

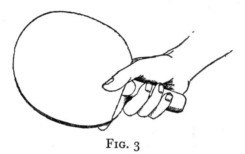

FIG. 3

Hold the blade between thumb and forefinger, with the thumb one side and the forefinger on the other, clasping the remaining fingers around the handle. Do not hold the bat too loosely or too tightly. If the hold is loose, you lose control over the bat; if the hold is too tight, it will strain the muscles of the arm.

The essential thing is that when playing forehand strokes the pressure is on the forefinger; for the backhand, the pressure is on the thumb.

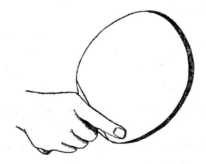

FIG. 4. Forehand, pressure on forefinger

19

FIG. 5. The backhand grip, pressure by thumb

I have always advocated, and still advocate, especially with Europeans, the use of the orthodox grip because it comes more naturally to them and it has a number of advantages. The main advantage is that less footwork is needed to cover the whole of the table all the time; it will also be found that the proper forehand and backhand strokes come easily with this grip.

With the penholder grip the forehand is the accepted stroke with which the player will score most of his points, as he is playing with one side of his bat. Just as the orthodox grip comes naturally to the Europeans, so does the penholder grip come naturally to the East Asians. After all, they hold the sticks with which they eat the same way as they hold a bat, so it is obvious that the penholder grip is absolutely natural to them.

Nevertheless, I must admit there is something to be said for the opinion that a penholder finds hitting easier and more natural. Just take a bat in your hand, holding it penholder-wise, and your first reaction is that you want to hit the ball; whereas, using the 'shake-hands' modern grip, you instinctively feel an impulse to push the ball back instead of clouting it. Yes, hitting comes to a penholder quite naturally. It is also true that because he has only the one grip, a penholder can hit faster and make up his mind more quickly what to do and how to do it, while an orthodox player has to decide whether to take the ball backhand or forehand, which, in most cases, means slight alterations of the grip. So the penholder has quite an advantage, if you think of it that way!

However, the advocates of the penholder grip quite forget to point out that, generally speaking, the backhand of people who use it is very poor, sometimes non-existent, and the same goes for defence. I have heard it argued that defence is not needed because reasonably accurate attack and counter-attack is usually good enough to beat anybody.

There is one rule, though, which is very important indeed, whether you use one grip or the other, that is, you must hold the blade and *not the handle*. Holding the bat by the blade will give you far better control and really this is the most important factor when learning the game. Once you acquire a bad habit it is difficult to change, therefore I again emphasize: hold the blade and *not the handle*.

5

Stance

Generally speaking, few people would think that a special section is needed to describe what sort of position a player, especially a beginner should take up when playing table tennis. However, I have seen so many beginners start off with the wrong stance that I believe it is absolutely necessary to discuss this matter in some detail.

A well-balanced position with the feet, one which is comfortable, ought to be almost automatic. However, lots of people begin by standing in a position which is both strained and unnatural (for some curious reason this applies especially to women), with the result that it is quite impossible to play strokes correctly. They are off balance and cannot move quickly and smoothly in the required direction.

Take up your position approximately 18 in from the table, feet parallel with the net and the table, and slightly apart, knees bent just a little and your weight thrown slightly forward. From this position you can quickly cover the whole of the table and can turn with equal facility for forehand or backhand as the ball comes at your right or to your left. It is quite easy to move forward or backward with little effort.

Your natural stance must be very nearly square, but as soon as the ball leaves your opponent's bat (and even before, when in course of time you have acquired a sense of anticipation) face one way or the other according to whether you intend to play the ball on the forehand or on the backhand. Left foot forward *slightly*, left shoulder pointing towards the net if a forehand shot is intended, right foot and right shoulder forward if a backhand stroke is to be played. A left-handed player would reverse these positions. The body must be mobile; the movements cannot be easy without a perfect balance and by putting your weight either on one foot or on the other, you will be able to move in whatever direction is required.

FIG. 6. Basic stance

After completing your stroke immediate recovery must be made to the original natural stance so that freedom of movement will come easily for the next stroke. A good player is ready for any eventuality at any time, the indifferent player will not be.

A proper stance is the beginning of proper footwork with which I will deal later on.

6

Service and Return of Service

It might be a good thing to go back to the history of the service, as we did in the case of the bat.

The rules of service were originally very simple and easy, and although almost everyone could take a small advantage from the service by putting spin into it *with the bat*, it was not very difficult for a good player to handle it. However, around the middle of the 1930's, the Americans brought in the dreaded so-called 'finger-spin' which nearly ruined the game. The name 'finger-spin' is practically self-explanatory; it means that the spin to the ball was put in by a whip of the fingers as certain bowlers do in cricket.

The Americans were the first to develop 'finger-spin' to such an extent that it was practically impossible for any player, even a champion, to return the service with any accuracy. So, there were then players who really could not play the game very well but had terrific finger-spin service and so could beat the best in the world. The game became quite farcical.

This compelled the International Table Tennis Federation to change the rules, and today the advantages gained by the service are very limited, provided that umpires make certain that the rules are obeyed. The rules lay down that the ball should be placed on the palm of the free hand which must be stationary and above tne level of the playing surface. The server shall commence the service by projecting the ball by hand only, without imparting spin, nearly vertically upwards so that the ball is visible at all times to the umpire, and so that it visibly leaves the palm. As the ball is descending from the height of its trajectory it shall be struck so that it first touches the server's court and then passes over or around the net and touches the receiver's court.

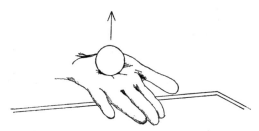

FIG. 7. Open palm above line of table. Ball thrown upwards

So the rules are quite simple. Nevertheless, with its limited advantages, the service plays a big part in the game. It must not be said that it is merely a means of putting the ball into play. Even if you do not win a service outright it is important that the service should be considered the forerunner of the game you want to follow.

Variety is absolutely necessary; try not to use the same service all the time. Vary the length, serving short ones or long ones according to whether your opponent is very near, or far away from the table, so as to make him lose his balance. With some services include some chops, with others rather more speed; keep your opponent guessing as to your intentions, never letting him know whether your ball will go just over the net or to the far end of the table. Serving just to the middle is usually less effective.

Speed is also very important and if you can serve with the same speed as you would use for a normal hit, so much the better. Aim and practise for this. Also look to see how you can take advantage by serving on your opponent's backhand or forehand side.

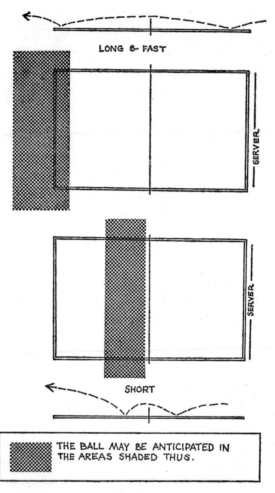

LONG & FAST

SERVER

SERVER

SHORT

THE BALL MAY BE ANTICIPATED IN
THE AREAS SHADED THUS.

FIG. 8

Just one more thing—the service is part of the game and should be practised as much as any other stroke. Furthermore, you must get into the habit of watching your opponent and not the table, bat or ball. This applies to every part of the game but it is with the service that you begin your 'know how'.

What about receiving service! Just as serving needs some cunning and intelligence, so does receiving need full attention and concentration.

Your balance while waiting for the service is essential. You must be ready to go either forward, sideways or backwards without losing your balance and be ready for the next stroke. Every server hopes that you will either miss the service or you will give a 'sitter', or else you will lose your balance so that his next hit will be a winner. The Asians are very good at disappointing such hopes, and I see no reason why Europeans also should not gain all possible advantage.

My advice to you on returning a service is to put some cut into it which makes it rather difficult for the opponent to hit an outright winner. However, if you are caught at the end of the table and the oncoming service is a fast one, and you have no time to go back, then the other alternative is to return a half-volley. There again, try to watch your opponent and put the service back to that part of your opponent's court where it is less likely that he can take advantage of it, i.e. out of his reach or straight to his body. Watching your opponent rather than the ball will give you that little advantage so much needed.

In so many sports it is said that a player should watch the ball. This might be true for the beginner but we are aiming higher and, as I said, this is the time to learn the real essentials. Watching your opponent instead of the ball—if you can do it—is a must.

7

The Half-Volley

The half-volley has become the basic stroke of modern table tennis. It is difficult to imagine any player reaching a great height today without this stroke, although the stroke itself is one of the simplest, needing only a little practice and getting the feel of the bat.

It is interesting to recall that the half-volley was originally the foundation of the game and that it lost some of its importance as long-range play took its place. Now with the advent of the sponge bat it is again more important than any other stroke I can think of.

This is the result of different types of materials being used, so that the bats give more significance to faster returns. A quick return can disturb the opponent greatly and the defensive player has less time to retreat from the table. In these circumstances, the half-volley is possibly the best stroke which can be employed.

FIG. 9. Half-volley

For those who are not familiar with the half-volley I had better explain that this is a stroke in which ball, bat and table meet at the same time, the ball not being allowed to come up. In fact, the ball is pressed between table and bat and the angle of the bat to the table determines the speed and the direction of the ball. If the oncoming ball is very fast it is necessary to close the angle between the table and the bat; on the other hand, if the ball is somewhat slow, the angle should be opened at the point of impact.

As I have said, it is fairly easy to learn the stroke but not quite so easy to play it well. A good reflex is necessary, as all depends on the quickness of eye and hand.

Using the face of the bat, place it with the edge of the blade almost touching the table so that the ball strikes it immediately after it bounces. The angle of the blade depends on the pace of the oncoming ball; the blade is slanted forward if the ball is fast, and the angle opens if it is slow. I think I can express myself better if I use the words closed and open instead of forward and back. After that it is only a matter of practice and growing experience to find out how much closing and opening of the angle is required to return safely shots of different strength. As it is a matter of experience, the movement later becomes automatic.

In the half-volley the bat intercepts the ball at the very beginning of its upward bounce. The bat is simply placed in the path of the ball in such a way that it rebounds by its own momentum. One thing to remember is not to 'push' the ball forward, especially if it is a fast one. Furthermore, once the ball is rising, a half-volley shot becomes impossible; it is absolutely imperative, therefore, that the bat should be put quickly where the ball hits the table.

I have not talked yet of the chop or cut, but never use the half-volley against these strokes. It is a dead certainty that if you do the ball will finish in the net, because of the peculiar spin imparted by the chop. Therefore against a chop you must go well

29

under the ball which obviously is not done in the case of a half-volley.

To sum up, these are the main points: open the angle for a slow ball, close the angle of the bat when half-volleying a fast ball. If anything, jerk your hand backwards rather than push when dealing with a very hard hit. This movement will deaden the hit considerably—consequently, the hardest smash can be returned with a half-volley. Never use the shot against a chop.

8

The Chop (or Cut) and Counter-Chop

When an absolute beginner goes to the table and starts to play he will probably let the ball bounce and just tap it back. I do not think there is anything else he would attempt to do.

This pit-pat or ping-pong is called the '*push stroke*' and many people talk and write a great deal about it. I hate to be different but I believe that this stroke should be disregarded completely, and I only distinguish two strokes: the half-volley, which I have already talked about, and the chop. The reason I disregard the push stroke is that it does not serve any purpose whatsoever and as I have said several times before in this book, it is far better to begin and learn the game properly and not to change strokes later on.

The chop is a very important and useful stroke which has tended recently to be neglected. The trend today is to hit, and a chop is supposed to be a defensive stroke. Therefore beginners and most players go out to hit, which is correct, but what can you do if hitting or counter-hitting results in a losing game or your opponent just will not let you hit? The chop is the answer, and the better the chop the more difficult an opponent you become. Perfect it as much as you can and you will possess a very excellent weapon.

For a good effective chop the bat has to be taken fairly high and the movement of the arm is downwards. The more the movement is downwards rather than forward, the better will be the result. The ball should be taken on its upward bounce because if it is left too late and is already dropping, you will have to 'scoop', with far less effective result. The properly played chop will not bounce high enough on the other side of the table to be hit with any force by your opponent. Another way to describe the stroke would be to say that you slice or cut the '*back*' of the ball.

FIG. 11. Chop backhand

FIG. 10. Chop forehand

That is why it is called chop or cut. This so-called cut gives tremendous back-spin to the ball, hence the low bounce and consequent difficulty in hitting it. If you merely touch the ball it will automatically go to the bottom of the net.

Although the chop is mainly a defensive stroke, I believe it can be used very aggressively as well. The stroke must not be just a means to get the ball back, but it should have some bite in it, producing a problem for the opponent.

To chop with little effect is comparatively easy; on the other

32

1. The Author coming in from behind the table with a long jump
to smash a poorly placed drop shot

2. The Author captaining the English Team, together with Diana Rowe and Ann-Haydon-Jones who won the European Team Championship in Budapest, 1958

hand the learning of a really good chop is not at all easy, because the extra bite is given with a flick of the wrist and to learn that flick is very difficult indeed. The way to improve your chop is to persevere. Try to chop harder and harder until eventually you will notice that one of your chops is more effective than another; feel your way through continued practice to a perfect shot.

Personally, I was not merely a defensive player yet my chop got me out of a lot of trouble. In spite of the fact that the trend today is attack I have no doubt that an all-round game is the best and it is then up to you whether you want to hit, defend or do both.

To make the chop more effective, take the ball as early as possible. Spooning the ball from below the table is not so effective, it is more likely to provide your opponent with a 'sitter'. An added advantage can be obtained by varying the strength of the chop. If your chop is always the same but has a different strength every time you do it, then your opponent will be confused, never knowing how much to lift it, with the result that he will make many mistakes.

Once you have mastered this stroke and you know how to put it to its best use, you will realize that it pays good dividends. A well-returned chop is far more effective than the original chop and there are many first-class players who just do not know how to handle them. There are so many players who are used to attack and counter-attack who are baffled by a sudden chop.

How would you deal with this chop? Generally people attack them, that is try to lift them. If the chop is a poor one the attacking player at the other side has very little difficulty. On the other hand, if it is a real chop with plenty of bite in it, a hard hit is out of the question; the answer is to lift the ball, and you just have to learn to feel how much strength you should put into your lift and how hard you can hit it.

As I said, if the chop is hard then the only thing you can do is

c

to lift it gently; in which case, the chopper has an easy task. Furthermore, if your lift is high he can easily attack it. The other way to deal with a chop is to 'counter-chop' it; that is, you play back a spin with another back-spin, returning the ball by putting your bat well *below the level of the table*, holding the bat horizontally.

FIG. 12. Chopping a back-spin

The difference between the chop and the counter-chop is that you chop with a downward movement, holding the bat half vertically, but for a counter-chop you make the stroke holding the bat absolutely horizontal. There is also more forearm and wrist action on the counter-chop than in the chop itself.

9

Attack—the Forehand

Every player who aims to be a champion must know how to attack. Although in the history of the game there have been one or two players who achieved the world title by playing mainly a defensive game, as a general rule attacking or all-round players achieve the greatest honours.

When you are a beginner and you play in a lower class, defensive play can succeed mainly by your opponent's mistakes, but when you get into a higher class, you must know how to score points, otherwise you are at the mercy of your opponent, who can slow down his game in order not to make mistakes, when he sees that you are not going to attack. The basic rule for all types of attack is that the movement of the arm is always 'upwards'. This applies both to forehand and backhand or counter-attack.

Without exception, people find it much easier to play a forehand than a backhand. Why? The answer is that this is the stroke which comes naturally because there is so much room to execute it.

For playing a forehand, place your left foot forward in front of your right foot, left shoulder facing the net and in the same continuous line with the left foot. The main thing is that you should stand sideways to achieve perfect rhythm and timing. There can be a free-sweeping movement of the arm without imparing the action. To produce the stroke correctly, position yourself first

35

before hitting the ball. Standing sideways, by the way, applies to every stroke and this is the secret of a consistent game.

Do not stand still; if possible keep moving all the time, turning to one side or the other according to the stroke you use. This is very important; everybody can assume the proper stance at the beginning of play, but from that point they do not always turn enough for a backhand or forehand. Another important point: go to the ball, do not reach for it, and should the ball come to you, move away to take up exactly the position you like and which suits you best.

FIG. 13

Most people have a certain distance from which they like to hit the ball; so if the ball is going away from you go nearer to it. If it comes to you, move away from it. Always look for the distance you like, which means, as I said before, that you should move continually. Hit the ball early as it goes upward or when it reaches the top of its rise; never hit it when it is falling.

Although all forehand shots seem to be alike, there is a slight difference between a lift, a loop and a kill-shot. With the lift, you play the ball fairly early on the rise to make sure not to miss. With the 'kill', the thing is not to wait for the ball to reach the top of its bounce before you start your own hitting movement. Impact, however, must be made at the top of the bounce so that you have the biggest possible target at which to aim. Furthermore, you should put the weight of your whole body behind a kill.

Another point is that the farther you are away from the table the longer should be the swing of the playing arm. The movement is much shorter when closer to the table.

Now I would like to give you one or two hints which might be useful to you later on. You should aim your 'kill'-shot to the place where your opponent least expects it. Therefore you must disguise your hit. How? For a right-handed player the left shoulder is the rudder, so to speak. If your left shoulder is in front, obviously you cannot hit across the table, you will hit straight down the line, which an experienced player will be able to detect immediately. On the other hand, most people have their left shoulder well back, which means they are going to hit across the table. The way to disguise your hit is to change the position of your left shoulder in the last possible second. This is not easy, but if you understand what I am trying to tell you, and practise a little, you will be surprised at your success.

It is fairly easy to hit either to one side or the other side of the table; it is far more difficult to hit to the centre because the trajectory of the ball is less, and it is therefore easier to make mistakes. Here again, one must hit down *'to the body'*, where the opponent will find it far more difficult to make a return.

I never forget my experiences when I was captain of the English ladies' team in one of the World Championships; England played China in the Team Championship. Ann-Haydon-Jones was play-

37

ing the Chinese number one. Ann won the first set easily but after that I saw the Chinese team going into a huddle and giving some advice to their girl. Consequently, instead of hitting to Ann's backhand to stop her using her match-winning forehand, the Chinese girl was aiming every shot to the middle of the table—to Ann's body—and in this way she succeeded in winning the second set. I therefore told Ann to go to the left or the right corner but never to stand in the middle, and the tactics paid off as she won the third and final set. Unfortunately for Ann and for us, the two girls met also in the quarter finals of the individual singles, when the Chinese girl went one better; she was not hitting to the middle but to wherever Ann went, that is, straight to her body. Ann did not know what to do, neither could I advise her to do anything except to try to stop the Chinese girl from hitting. It was not Ann's game at all, so she had to concede defeat. I have said all this just to illustrate my point and hope that something can be learned from it.

The loop is part of the forehand stroke, used fairly widely today. The difference between the lift and the loop is that in the lift the ball is hit with a split-second impact, the arm following through and ending above the head, whereas with the loop the stroke begins about knee high, the ball being taken later than usual as it drops away. The bat comes up vertically with very little forward movement and the action should be slow at first with a very short increase in the speed of the bat just before contacting the ball, which will impart the maximum amount of top-spin. The result is that the ball will then travel forward comparatively slowly, though when it touches the other side of the table the character of the spin causes the ball to bite into the table surface which results in its going forward and upward with unexpected acceleration. The main advantage of the loop drive is that it enables the player to force the opponent away from the table unless he is good at returning it at half-volley.

When learning you will probably find that you cannot put sufficient spin on to the ball, but my advice is that you should practise it, and if you have a natural aptitude the stroke will come. If it does not suit your style, do not worry. Table tennis has plenty of strokes and tremendous variety waiting at your disposal.

The Backhand

This is supposed to be a far more difficult stroke than the fore-hand, and even among present-day champions, very few indeed have a very good backhand. To me this is difficult to understand, for I prefer to use my backhand, and have always found it easy.

The difference between forehand and backhand is that while most forehand players find plenty of room in front of the body to make that movement, when playing a backhand there is little or no room at all, because the body and especially the left shoulder is in the way. The thing to do is to put the right foot forward together with the right shoulder, but even more important, to keep the left foot and the left shoulder well back; that is, to take up exactly the opposite position to that for the forehand, which will enable you to have the same freedom of movement for the backhand as you would have for the forehand. I repeat, *left shoulder and left foot well back*, and there you have it.

My own reason for using it so much is that a backhand is mainly played with the forearm, while the forehand is mostly played from the shoulder, and so I found it more economical to use my forearm than my full arm. Furthermore, as you play the stroke from the forearm you have more chance to disguise the direction of your shot. The intended direction is hard to detect, and there is the added advantage that you can make up your mind far later, at the last possible second, as to where you are going to place the ball.

Otherwise the points to remember about the forehand apply equally to the backhand: one foot in front of the other, the movement of arm upwards, never hit the ball when it is falling and remember that right shoulder and right foot move always together just as left foot and left shoulder move together. If you try to move with your foot leaving your shoulder behind, or vice versa, it just will not do.

FIG. 14. Backhand

Making a loop drive from the backhand is more difficult than from the forehand and there are only a few players in the world who even attempt to make a backhand loop. The explanation is that while making a forehand loop the *wrist* must bend inwards, while for a backhand loop, the wrist should bend the other way. Try to bend your wrist in different directions even without bat and ball—you will find you cannot bend it as far *out* as *in*. Obviously, the backhand loop must be, and is, more difficult and less effective.

I I

The Counter-Attack

Counter-attack is just as much a part of the game as any other stroke, and must not be looked upon as something different. Some players use this stroke as a do or die effort when they seem to have no alternative; but this should not be so. It should be used regularly as the situation demands it.

It follows that the counter-attack should not be regarded as a haphazard hit or miss effort. Concentrate on a good directional aim rather than sheer force; wild hitting is not much use and in the long run loses more points than it gains. The stroke production is exactly the same as for attack; footwork, movement of arm, etc., are the same; the great difference lies in the timing.

There are two types of counter-attack; one is the half-volley counter-attack which is used nowadays far more frequently than before, and the other one, taken far away from the table, is exactly like the backhand and forehand except that the movement of the arm is much longer and even for the backhand the ball is hit from the shoulder, with the full arm and not with the fore-arm.

First let us deal with the half-volley counter-attack. Just as with the half-volley, you must not let the ball bounce and you must hit it back before it begins its rise from the table. The difference is that while with the half-volley you just put your bat in the path of the ball, when counter-attacking you start your movement practically at the time when the ball leaves your opponent's racket;

42

that is, you swing the bat instead of just putting it on the table. The timing is crucial and this requires a little anticipation which will come with practice.

This stroke has become an exceedingly important one since the introduction of the sponge bat and the loop drive, as these both make returning with a half-volley easier than letting the ball bounce. For many years people were reluctant to use this stroke as it looks difficult, but really and truly it is a fairly simple stroke. Try not to use the wrist except to give direction to the hit.

The counter-attack from far away from the table is no different from any other stroke except that the stance will be farther back from the table to allow perfect freedom of movement. The ball should not be hit flat; give it as much top-spin as you can put into it. The better the top-spin the less likelihood there is of the receiver being able to hit it back, at least with any degree of accuracy. As for backhand and forehand, stand sideways, and try not to hurry.

The longer you take to play a shot the more time you will have to pick out the best point at which to place the ball, with the added advantage that, as far as placing goes, you can be more consistent.

As I mentioned before, a haphazard, wild hit will go wrong almost every time.

When to counter-attack? This is difficult to put on paper as you must judge the stance, the position and the situation of your opponent. However, it is easier to tell you against which types of players the counter-attack should be employed. First of all, against an opponent who cannot defend, only hit. If you hit first or you can successfully counter-attack, the tactic will probably pay dividends, but you must be cautious and not indulge in bashing, in other words you must not counter-attack all the time, because probably your opponent, who knows only how to hit and counter-attack, is better at playing that sort of game.

Just worry him, so that he cannot wait, and try to force him into errors.

Another type of player against whom the counter-attack should be used is the one whose reactions are slow. I mean a player who is quite good if you allow him to play his own game but who is disturbed when faced with the unexpected. Counter-attack also against players with poor balance. Here I mean those who put too much body behind a stroke and are slow to recover their original stance.

Use the counter-attack if you are in trouble, if you are badly placed or have lost your balance. You must also use the counter-attack against players who are weak on one wing, and are covering the whole of the table from one corner. They are very vulnerable to counter-attack, which, among other things, will force them from their favourite position.

12

The Drop-Shot

There is a stroke in table tennis which I am sure everybody uses; this is the drop-shot, but whilst some people make the most of it, others use it less effectively. Even to the best and easiest of hitters a drop-shot is essential. Concentrated hitting by itself can pay off well but it is likely to be more effective when interspersed with drop-shots.

For one thing, even nowadays when play is close to the table, it is evident that long-range defence is still one of the features of the game. Therefore it is when players go away from the table to return deep drives that the drop-shot should be brought into use by the attacker.

The shot should be used first and foremost to win points or to force the defender to come back to the table, often to abandon his favourite position, upsetting his balance. There is a strong psychological as well as physical aspect to this stroke. When a player is made to realize that his attacking opponent has a habit of mixing drop-shots with his hits, he begins to worry as to how far he dare retreat from the table. He might become reluctant to go as far as he would like to, and probably be rattled by his opponent's tactics. He must be ready at all times to jump forward to tackle a drop-shot. Try to introduce the element of surprise and keep him on the move backwards and forwards. He will expend a great deal of energy, possibly more than he can afford in a very hard-fought game.

45

The drop-shot is best used when the ball drops close to your side of the net, which will enable you to drop it back gently just over to the other side of the net. The way to do it by a half-volley is with the angle of the bat slightly opened. The important point is that you should not push the ball with your bat and it should be played delicately.

As you will know by now, most half-volleys are played from the backhand. Nevertheless, for a good drop-shot I would recommend the use of a forehand half-volley, for the following reasons:

Firstly, you get a better 'feel' as to how much angle and touch to apply, and secondly, it is easier to disguise your intentions as to whether you are going to use a drop-shot or carry on hitting, as so many players use their forehand more than their backhand. Later, with a little experience, you will find it quite easy to realize whether your opponent is going to hit or use a drop-shot, because when a forehand hit is being made, the shoulders rise as the body is put into the shot. The intention to play a drop-shot can be noticeable by the fact that your opponent drops his shoulders just before making it.

Keep these points in mind when you are making a drop-shot. Do not advertise your intention by dropping your shoulders, this is the clearest of all indications that you are not going to hit the ball. Pretend that you are preparing to hit and move your shoulders accordingly, drop it in the last possible moment.

There are other points which one should keep in mind. One of them is that 'the middle of the table' is the best place to put the ball, because if the stroke is correct and well executed, the ball will bounce at least twice on the table before dropping. However, if the ball is angled it might bounce over the side of the table and it will be easier to reach it before it hits the floor. So do not angle your drop-shot, play down to the middle.

Another point: if possible use the stroke when your opponent is in the process of moving away from the table; when one is

46

stationary, however far from the table, it is easier to run in to get a drop-shot than it is to reach one when moving away from the table. If you want to get your opponent on the wrong foot, your best bet is to sell a dummy when he is back-pedalling.

FIG. 15. Drop-shot

The drop-shot requires good judgement of pace and touch, played badly it can be dangerous because its failure to produce the desired effect may give a quick-footed player the opportunity to switch from defence to attack. A bad drop-shot usually turns out to be a 'sitter' close to the net which can hardly be missed by your opponent. I can give you some advice here, although it does not relate to the drop-shot alone—'Do not carry the bat in front of you'—if you do so it is obvious that you will not be able to hit the ball; the most you can do is to return it.

If you keep your bat in a position close to your body or even behind it, then you will not only be able to return a drop-shot or any ball for that matter, but will be ready to hit or play any shot you decide to make. So keep your bat near to your body!

47

13

Footwork

I am sure most of you have seen table-tennis stars performing either on television, in your club or at tournaments. Unfortunately there are a number of them who have taken up a new style where footwork is concerned. I do not want to mention names, but the fact is that they are standing square to the table and hitting every ball right or left without moving their feet very much. Sometimes they win because of their marvellous ball control where their hands are concerned, but sometimes they lose by reason of their inability to play shots correctly and consistently, because of their lack of footwork. You may know every stroke in the textbook, but in my opinion there is little hope of reaching the very top without adequate footwork.

Earlier, under the heading of Stance, I stated that you should try to avoid standing square to the table. Of course your natural waiting stance must be very nearly square, but as soon as the ball leaves your opponent's bat, move one way or the other, depending on whether you are to make a forehand or a backhand shot. This applies to both attack and defence, but in playing backhand or forehand, it is essential that the appropriate foot should be a little in advance of the other. After completing the stroke an immediate recovery must be made back to the natural stance so that you are prepared to turn in any direction at a fraction of a second's notice.

In talking about footwork I must emphasize that it is not a

48

3. The Author jumping like a goal-keeper to return a hard hit ball
practically out of his reach

4. A view of the playing arena of a World Championship during the
preliminary rounds

question of moving the feet only. The movement of the shoulders must be synchronized exactly with body movement and balance. Shoulder and foot go together, that is, if the left foot goes back then the left shoulder must go back with it. If the right shoulder goes back then the right foot must go back also. This applies, of course, not only when going backwards but when moving in any direction or into any position when you are about to make your stroke. This is not only a recommended way to play but also the correct way.

I think you will understand this better if you try just the opposite. Move your foot in one direction and leave your shoulder pointing in the other direction, or vice versa, and you will see that it is quite impossible to achieve a proper stroke. By trying to do the wrong thing, you will realize straight away the correct way of playing and the importance of footwork.

Another thing you should try to learn straight away is to play with both of your feet. It is absolutely amazing that even amongst the best players you find people who cannot use *both* their feet equally well; they usually stay on the left foot and move their right foot around it. You should be able to do the same thing with the other foot, that is, to keep your right foot where it is and move the left foot if and when it is necessary.

When turning from a forehand to a backhand, for instance, with your left foot in front, you will probably put your right foot and right shoulder forward first and only later move your left side backward. This involves two movements whereas if you could simply move your left foot backward this would necessitate only one move to get to the same position. Do not be discouraged if at first you find this difficult. As I have said, even the best players, because of force of habit, find it difficult to change their style.

This is a great handicap when turning from one stroke to another is concerned. Players generally seem to be weak on the

D   49

backhand and this is simply because they are unable to move quickly enough into position. This is basically the fault of the feet.

Never keep your feet too far apart because this is a difficult stance from which to start any movement, as it makes it hard to shift the balance from one foot to another. If you have your feet closer together it is much easier to transfer the weight from left to right and vice versa.

If you have to run to the ball then run and do not shuffle. Take your feet off the floor and do not be afraid to lift from the knee.

When going for a short service do not lunge forward with the bat. Go forward first on your foot and then put the bat to the ball. Not only do you make a better return but you will be able to keep your balance.

You should be moving all the time. When you make a stroke, hit while moving with the ball. Every player has his right distance from which to hit the ball; you must always, therefore, try to find that distance with your feet.

To summarize the principles involved: when playing a stroke first move with your feet then with your bat. Do not be afraid that you won't have time to get to the ball, as you will soon be able to adjust your stroke and instead of having little time to make a return, you will find that you have more time at your disposal. A good player can always be distinguished from a poor one by the greater amount of time the former has in which to make a stroke.

Do not get the idea that you need more footwork for defence than for attack. Move just as much and as far to an attacking position as you expect to do when defending.

Do try to go to the ball all the time, and should it come to you, or be hit at you, then move away from it, always remembering that turning sideways is the way to make a correct return.

14

Anticipation

It is not an empty claim that anticipation is a natural gift and that it is not something which one can develop easily, if it does not come naturally. Nevertheless, I believe that one can learn or acquire a certain amount of anticipation by sheer observation and by watching your opponent closely instead of looking for the ball.

I have already explained, when discussing the drop-shot, that you can tell what your opponent will do by the way he carries his bat. If it is too much in front of him it will be impossible for him to hit.

There are other things, too, from which you can learn a lot about your opponent's intentions. First of all, look at your opponent's *shoulders*, especially the non-playing one. That is, if he is right-handed, watch his left shoulder. If it is well back then you can expect him to hit across the table, if the shoulder is well in front of him, then the hit will be a straight one down to the line. This applies to both the forehand and the backhand. Naturally what every good player tries to do is to deceive you by switching the movement of the shoulder in the last possible moment, so that is the thing you must look out for and which you must do yourself when playing a stroke.

The main thing is to watch your opponent all the time. Many people believe that the important thing is to watch the ball. I can never agree with this view, because provided you are playing on a good table and with a good ball, there is no need to watch the bounce of the ball; you will know it by heart. It is far more important to learn when and where to hit the ball.

I used to play football a lot and I was taught the game by a very famous coach. He used to tell me that there is one great difference between a top-class player and an average player. An average player will look at the ball at his feet hardly knowing where his colleagues are, while a top-class player will just take one look at the ball, his main concern being to look for his colleagues and watch the field. I knew my coach was right, it was not difficult for me to adopt the same tactics for table tennis.

15

The Human Element and Temperament

I have had a long career as a table tennis player and have also coached a little, mainly friends and national teams, because I enjoyed it. Now I know that at times, especially earlier on, I used to make a fatal mistake.

Very often I found a young boy or girl whose general play, hitting and defence, amazed me, and I was sure he or she would go very far. It was only later on that I realized that talent alone is not enough. Unless you have the will, fighting spirit, intelligence, etc., which I call the personality element, however talented you are, you are not going to make it. Therefore, I think that table tennis, unlike swimming or running where natural talent perhaps counts more, is one of the games in which I would place personality before talent. The explanation is simple; if you are talented but have not got the fighting spirit and will to win, then there is nothing a coach or anybody else can do.

On the other hand, very often if you are intelligent enough, have a reasonable physique and a determined personality, then in spite of your lack of talent you can become a great player. In simple terms, if you have talent only, nobody can give you the rest, but it is not so very difficult to teach you everything that comes easily to the talented player, if you have the will to learn it.

Temperament also comes under the heading of human element. You must discipline yourself and even if you happen to

53

be a person with a temper, you can teach yourself to be otherwise.

Here too, I speak from personal experience, because as a young boy I was a terribly bad loser, which cost me many games. However, I taught myself to control my feelings, and smiled even when I ought to have cried. Please do not get me wrong, though; I do not want you to be a good loser who would smile not caring whether he lost or won; all I ask you to do is not to show that you care. Keep your feelings within yourself and always try to think how you can keep your advantage or get out of trouble.

There are a number of points which are more tangible. First, do not be upset if the umpire makes a mistake; it can happen to anyone. Try to understand that this is part of the game; do not argue with him. If your opponent scores with a net-ball or an edge-ball, again do not be upset. This too is part of the game and you may presently find yourself doing the same thing. These things have a way of averaging out.

Above all be a sportsman; do not look for excuses and do not fall to an opponent who indulges in gamesmanship and similar tricks. He may do it because he cannot help it or he may do it purposely to upset your rhythm. If you get upset he has achieved his aim and you are playing into his hands. So keep cool, just play table tennis and whatever happens, try to smile. I know it is not easy but you can train yourself. Furthermore, a player who can smile under any circumstances is more frightening to an opponent; surely it must shake his confidence.

Where fighting spirit is concerned, the important thing is to fight from beginning to end. Do not start lightheartedly or ease off because you have a good lead. A good start will give you confidence and that is no comfort to your opponent; keep it that way. On the other hand, should you happen to be losing think that *while you are at the table* you have still got a chance to win, but if you just throw it away or give in, you have no chance at all.

54

Never make excuses or look for them or try to invent them; they are absolutely valueless.

Just a final point: I have always believed, and still do, in honesty. You must play according to the rules and although you can take advantage of your opponent's weaknesses you must still be a fair-minded sportsman. This means that if the umpire happens to make a mistake in your favour, you should put him right, even if your opponent does not do this. Your successes will be sweeter because well deserved. You will also have an extra incentive to do your utmost.

Hundreds of times I have been asked by players: 'As soon as I begin to play a serious match I get terribly frightened. What shall I do?'

To such people I have two tips to give. First, pay attention to your feet and try to move more, because the first sign of nervousness is that your feet seem glued to the ground, and if you occupy your mind with improving your footwork, your nervous tension will be released.

Secondly, have a good look at your opponent's face, more often than not he is just as anxious and worried as you!

16

Doubles

It is only natural that players should concentrate on singles play. After all, the singles title is the one every player seeks —and actually it is through the singles that a player's ability is measured.

Nevertheless, 'Doubles' plays a very important part in the game. In all tournaments doubles events are included and they are a vital part of the Women's World Team competition, the Corbillon Cup. Some countries realize the importance of doubles, teaching it and playing it regularly. Others tend to neglect it completely, taking it as a sideline and only playing it when they have to.

I have always maintained that a player should play as many doubles as possible, not only to improve his doubles play, but also to improve his knowledge of the whole game. Only doubles will give you that education which is so important to a great player, to know what one is doing, to anticipate what the opponents will do and sense the tactics which should be adopted in various circumstances.

So apart from being a great game, it is quite an education as well, especially when playing against better players. You can see their style, footwork, etc., from close up, having just a little extra time for observation.

I myself learned a lot by playing doubles and maintain that it is the reason I did as well as I did in my playing days. It is not necessarily the right assumption that good singles players make good doubles players as well.

What is the art of doubles play? It can be summed up in four points:

(1) Shield and protect your partner's weak and vulnerable points.
(2) Create opportunities to bring in your partner's best stroke.
(3) Take full advantage of any of the opponents' weaknesses.
(4) Assess and play the correct tactical game.

Of course, the first essential is to know your partner and be familiar with his or her strong points and weaknesses. If your partner is a hitter rather than a defender, you must force the game to help him to get in his hit. On the other hand, if he cannot hit it is not worth while to lift the ball because on the return he will

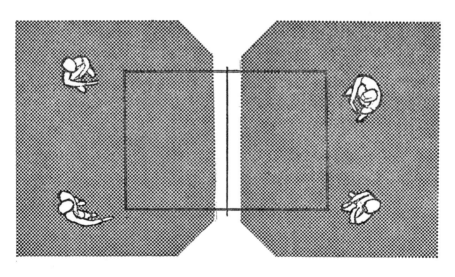

EACH PLAYER MUST BE PREPARED TO COVER THE SHADED AREA DURING A DOUBLES GAME, ENSURING FREEDOM OF MOVEMENT FOR HIS PARTNER.

Fig. 16

57

be unable to carry on the attack. In this case, you must try to hit decisively or chop hard because it is easier to hit a lift than a chop.

But it is far more important to 'foresee' *where* your stroke will be 'likely' to be returned. To do this one must have some understanding of the whole game. Let me explain. It is generally accepted, and it is true to say, that it is easier to hit a ball across the table than it is to hit down a straight line because when hitting across the table the trajectory of the ball is longer, and therefore there is less chance of making an error. It is not hard to visualize that this knowledge will greatly help a player not to handicap his partner in any circumstances.

When playing with a partner whose game you know well, you have no problem as to which side you should stand, but generally the best thing is to cover the table from behind. To achieve this you move out to either the right or left side after you have made your stroke, and move round and back behind your partner so that you are able to go in and cover the whole table ready for any eventuality when your turn comes again.

It is a simple movement although it is important that one should not be caught at one side of the table out of position, and that moving around does not interfere with the partner.

The ideal partnership almost certainly is a right-handed player and a left-handed player, for the simple reason that most people prefer forehands, consequently if they both play with the same hand they want the same corner of the table, constantly disturbing and worrying each other. A left-handed player and a right-handed player, both playing the same strokes, will prove to be the best partnership. The best example is our Rowe Twins, who were one of the best women's doubles pairs that the game has ever had.

Another good combination is a good forehand player partnering a strong backhander. There again, each player prefers and

58

has his own side of the table, each of them knowing perfectly well what is in his own mind as well as in that of his partner.

I strongly recommend to everybody, even to those who do not aspire to become good doubles players, to play a lot of doubles. It will help them in singles play in the long run.

As for doubles, I repeat, a good doubles player is one who can help his partner. As every other stroke is hit by your partner, it follows that you cannot win a doubles game by your own efforts alone. It is essentially a team game, not two individuals trying to do their best.

17

Coaching

Before saying anything else on the subject of coaching, I would like to say this to clubs, associations and others who are keen to give coaching to their players: do not appoint more than two coaches for any one player. All of us are different and all coaches have different methods and ideas. I have seen many players ruined by having too many coaches thrust upon them. If a new one appears from time to time it is not long before the youngster becomes quite bewildered and loses all conception of what is the best thing to do.

When young they can have one coach at the beginner stage and perhaps another one later on, but never more. On the other hand, there is a bit of advice I would like to give to young players: have full confidence in your coach. If you have not got that you are better off without one. But if you have full confidence in him and his ability you must trust him and obey him implicitly. He should know what is good for you and how he can improve your play.

Many times I have heard that in order to be a good coach one does not need to be a good player. I fully agree, where the initial beginner stage is concerned, but I beg to differ when it comes to a higher standard of play. I maintain that personal experience is absolutely essential. How can a coach know what goes on in the head of a player when he plays on the centre court or in the final of a big championship unless he himself has experienced the same test and felt the same emotions? Playing well in practice or in a minor event is a very different thing from playing for your country or in a tournament of similar status, when the all-important thing is knowing *when* to execute a stroke rather than *how*.

I am against mass coaching unless it is in the beginner stage. You can teach *en masse* such principles as, for example, that to hit is an upward movement of the arm, and that the movement for a defensive stroke is downward. But this method is very limited in its scope. Individual coaching is the best, and a good coach should find out his pupil's ability and then play his game around the strong points. A coach must know his pupil personally—his intelligence, how much he can understand and how much he can be taught.

'Feeding' should be avoided. It is not much good playing continuously, say, to the pupil's forehand when teaching this stroke. Anybody can hit a good forehand drive if he is told to stand sideways, left foot forward, left shoulder facing the net, and then has the ball put in just the right place for him to hit. It is far better to explain how to play the stroke and, if possible, when, and to let the player find out what is expected of him. This will improve, amongst other things, his concentration and anticipation, which after all are very important aspects of the game.

There are strokes which are more difficult to learn than others. The loop and taking the loop, the chop and taking the chop, are the strokes I consider the most difficult ones in modern table tennis. One cannot practise them enough.

The best time to improve your game is in the off season, during the summer. Do not give up the game at the end of the season; play on if you are keen to make progress.

The preceding section explained the importance of playing lots of doubles. As a rule, good players do not care to play against weaker opponents, but if you pair up regardless of comparative strength, you may be given a better chance to improve. Do not be afraid of playing against a weaker position. That is the time when you should put into practice the things you are trying out. A strong player will not allow you to play as you want to. A coach should, apart from helping stroke production, give confidence to a modest person, curb the ego of the conceited player, and above all teach each player to *think for himself* and rely on his own ability and judgement.

18

Fitness

Table tennis is a high-powered sport which needs concentration, energy, speed and stamina. A player must be a highly trained athlete if he is to be a successful competitor.

An average tournament calls for considerable lasting power because players are called upon to engage in a number of matches, progressively more testing, usually for two and sometimes three days, although some big tournaments are played no longer than a single day. So it is clear that the table tennis players must pay special attention to fitness.

How do you keep fit? Different sportsmen have different ideas. A footballer has to be fit practically all the year round, a boxer really just for the fight, and a table tennis player is in a position between the two, although special training is necessary for a great event which lasts for more than two or three days.

My personal preference is for running, walking and P.T., although during the off season other sports such as swimming, football, tennis, etc., are good enough to keep one in trim.

The process of getting into top gear must be slow and gradual. The main point to remember is to avoid exhaustion. If you do too much you will wear yourself out instead of doing yourself good. When preparing for a big tournament I used to start off with slow walks and occasional sprints for not more than twenty minutes. At a later stage I did less walking and more running for longer periods.

Building up in this way, you can make yourself really fit, but I repeat, do just as much as you can; do not exhaust yourself. When you run, run properly without dragging your feet, lift your knees high, body forward, kick your way from the ground when sprinting. P.T., showers and hot baths will help a great deal to round off your training.

Just as it is essential to keep fit in readiness for a tournament, so it is important to remain fit throughout the duration of it. When you have finished your matches do not stand about watching others; instead, prepare yourself for the following session or next day. You must be fit not only physically but mentally as well. Mental and physical fitness go together; one is of little use without the other. So relax whenever you can, if you do not have to be at the hall go home or somewhere where you can relax. Very often when the day of the final arrives, stamina and confidence are seen to be far more important than mere stroke production.

Of course there are many other things such as loosening up to be taken into consideration. Never start a match before you have had a few practice shots and loosening-up exercises. Failing to do this will mean a bad start, finding yourself dropping behind and losing your confidence.

To sum up, fine strokes alone are not in themselves winners. You have got to be fully fit, physically and mentally, and you must have the stamina to last you right through to the end. To ignore these facts is to invite defeat however brilliant your game. Even if your interest in table tennis is only in having fun, no one can deny that winning is more enjoyable than losing.

19

Practice

Not even a genius can reach the heights without practice. While I believe that talent counts for much, hard work and keenness make up for the lack of it. Secondly, particularly when you are still a beginner, play as much as possible for hours and hours; although this still applies even when you become efficient. Nothing can give you ball control like plenty of play.

When practising, use a method. Indulging in a purposeless 'knock-up' is ruinous because it tends to lead players out of the habit of concentrating.

I said practise with a method. There are various ways to do this. My own favourite system, when practising, was to play one stroke throughout a complete game, i.e., a cross-court backhand through one game, a backhand straight down to the line in the next game and another stroke or variations in another game. Of course I played in these various ways without letting my opponent suspect what I was up to, and still trying to do my very best to win.

This demanded the maximum of concentration and was a great help to me, in particular to my ball control and ability to hit from any angle to any place I desired. Naturally I have done the same where defensive play was concerned, selecting a spot to which I returned the ball consistently. In this way I quickly learned how to deal with different players who were stronger on one side than the other, which helped me to cope with emergencies.

E

Practice should be the medium through which to learn. Therefore, it is no good going on the table just for a game. To learn new strokes and to improve your old ones should be your plan for your practice. Try to play as you would play in a competition. The only difference is that while in a tournament you may have to change your plans, in a practice game you must stick to them because the object is to improve yourself. The more seriously you can play, the better it is, but if you happen to lose, the consequences are negligible.

The reason for trying to play as you would in a tournament is that when you are out to win, your muscles are tighter, your nervous tension is different, and unless you have practised playing in that way you might just as well not have practised at all. Generally, of course, it is a very good thing, and useful, to practise against better players than yourself. However, when you have passed the beginner stage, I suggest it is better to play against weaker players, because perfecting ball control and improving your strokes is the main reason for practice. A strong player forces his own game upon you; you can dictate your own play when playing against a weaker opponent.

Just one more point, practise very hard but always remember that you will do more harm than good if you play when you are tired. When tired take a rest. You must have the ability to concentrate, and when you are tired physically or mentally this is just not possible.

20

The Expedite System

For those readers who are not absolutely familiar with the game and its rules, I am giving the rules in the next chapter.

Basically, the laws are very simple and easy to understand. Nevertheless, there is one rule which is a very important one from the playing point of view; this is the Expedite System, and I think it might be just as well to go into this in detail and give you some ideas which might be very useful to you, together with the background of its history.

For a good number of years there were no rules as to how long a game should last. However, in the mid-thirties the defensive players were so much on top that a large number of matches resulted in long-drawn-out boring games. Even now there are players who just have not got the ability to hit, and rely on their defensive know-how. When two of them meet, it is inevitable that the game will be a long and uneventful one.

The International Table Tennis Federation first tried to get over this by making a rule which limited each game to 20 minutes and whoever led at the end of that time won the game. Later on this time was reduced to 15 minutes. Now, however, all this has been abandoned.

A new system initiated by the U.S. Table Tennis Association has been adopted which is called the 'Expedite System'. If the game lasts 15 minutes it is stopped, and subsequently instead of one player serving five times, service alternates between the two players, and if the rally does not end after the ball has been struck twelve times by the server, he loses the point. All subsequent games will also be played under this system. Now this rule not only makes the game far more interesting than it was previously but its exploitation needs special knowledge and a player, especially an all-round player, can gain a lot of advantage from it.

Very often an attacking player cannot get through his opponent's defence and loses in spite of the fact that his opponent has no notion as to how to score a point. In this case, it might be good tactics for the attacking player to play out the first game to the full 15 minutes, which will mean that in the following games his opponent will have to try to hit and score when serving, otherwise he will lose the point. This strategy is fairly well known to most players but as some young players may not know it, I thought I should mention it.

Another way you can exploit the law is that when it is your opponent's turn to score a point, you try to stop him from hitting a lift, loop or any other attacking stroke which you can *do consistently*. You must not make an error because this defeats the object.

One more tip. When you are trying to prevent your opponent from hitting, aim all your directed strokes to the weaker side of your opponent. No doubt he will try to make a desperate counter-attack stroke which will probably be ineffective, but in any case you must be ready for it.

When the expedite system is in force the game becomes a tactical battle.

The advice given above suggests in a general way the advantages which, with a bit of intelligence, you can get from the rule.

21

Laws of Table Tennis

SINGLES

THE TABLE

The table shall be rectangular in surface, 274 cm (9 ft) in length, 152·5 cm (5 ft) in width; it shall be supported in such a way that its upper surface shall be 76 cm (2 ft 6 in) above the floor and shall lie in a horizontal plane.

It shall be made of any material and shall yield a uniform bounce of not less than 22 cm (8¾ in) and not more than 25 cm (9¾ in) when a standard ball, preferably of medium bounce, is dropped from a height of 30·5 cm (12 in) above its surface.

The upper surface of the table shall be termed the 'playing surface'; it shall be matt, colour very dark, preferably dark green, with a white line 2 cm (¾ in) broad along each edge.

The lines at the 152·5 cm edges or ends of the playing surface shall be termed 'end lines'. The lines at the 274 cm edges or sides of the playing surface shall be termed 'side lines'.

THE NET AND ITS SUPPORTS

The playing surface shall be divided into two courts of equal size by a net running parallel to the end lines and 137 cm (4 ft 6 in) from each. The net, with its suspension, shall be 183 cm (6 ft) in length; its upper part along its whole length shall be 15·25 cm (6 in) above the playing surface; its lower part along the whole length shall be close to the playing surface. The net shall be suspended by a cord attached at each end to an upright post 15·25 cm (6 in) high; the outside limits of each post shall be 15·25 cm (6 in) outside the side line.

THE BALL

The ball shall be spherical. It shall be made of celluloid or a similar plastic, white and matt; it shall not be less than 37·2 mm (1·46 in) nor more than 38·2 mm (1·50 in) in diameter; it shall not be less than 2·40 gr (37 grains) nor more than 2·53 gr (39 grains) in weight.

THE BAT

The bat may be of any size, shape or weight. Its surface shall be dark coloured and matt. The blade shall be wood, continuous, of even thickness, flat and rigid. If the blade is covered on either side, this covering may be either:

of plain, ordinary pimpled rubber, with pimples outward, of a total thickness of not more than 2 mm; or—

of 'sandwich', consisting of a layer of cellular rubber surfaced by plain ordinary pimpled rubber—turned outwards or inwards—in which case the total thickness of covering of either side shall not be more than 4 mm.

When rubber is used on both sides of a bat, the colour shall be similar; when wood is used for either side, or for both sides, it should be dark, either naturally, or by being stained (not painted) in such a way as not to change the friction-character of its surface.

Note: The part of the blade nearest the handle and gripped by the fingers may be covered with cork or other materials for convenience of grip; it is to be regarded as part of the handle.

Note: If the reverse side of the bat is never used for striking the ball, it may all be of cork or any other material convenient

70

for gripping. The limitation of bat cover-materials refers only to the striking surface. A stroke with a side covered with cork or any other gripping surface would, however, be illegal and result in a lost point.

A GOOD SERVICE

The ball shall be placed on the palm of the free hand, which must be stationary and above the level of the playing surface. Service shall commence by the server projecting the ball by hand only, without imparting spin, nearly vertically upwards so that the ball is visible at all times to the Umpire and so that it visibly leaves the palm. As the ball is then descending from the height of its trajectory, it shall be struck so that it touches first the server's court and then, passing directly over or around the net, touch the receiver's court.

Note: Missed Service: If a player, in attempting to serve, misses the ball altogether, it is a lost point because the ball was in play from the moment it left his hand and a good service has not been made of the ball already in play.

A GOOD RETURN

A ball having been served or returned in play shall be struck so that it passes directly over or around the net and touches directly the opponent's court, provided that, if the ball, having been served or returned in play, returns with its own impetus over or around the net, it may be struck, while in play, so that it touches directly the opponent's court.

IN PLAY

The ball is in play from the moment at which it is projected from the hand in service until:

It has touched one court twice consecutively.

It has, except in service, touched each court alternately without having been struck by the bat intermediately.

71

It has been struck by either player more than once consecutively.

It has touched either player or anything that he wears or
carries, except his bat or his bat hand below the wrist.

On the volley it comes in contact with the bat or the bat
hand below the wrist.

It has touched any object other than the net, supports, or
those referred to above.

A LET

The rally is a let:

If the ball served in passing over the net touches it or its supports, provided the service either is otherwise good or is
volleyed by the receiver. (Definition: *The Volley*—If the ball
comes into contact with the bat or the bat hand, not
yet having touched the playing surface on one side of the net
since last being struck on the other side, it shall be said to
have been volleyed.)

If a service is delivered when the receiver is not ready, provided
always that he may not be deemed to be unready if he
attempts to strike at the ball.

If either player is prevented by an accident, not under his
control, from serving a good service or making a good return.

If either player loses the point owing to an accident not within
his control.

BALL FRACTURED IN PLAY

If the ball splits or becomes otherwise fractured in play, affecting
a player's return, the rally is a let. It is the umpire's duty to stop
play, recording a let, when he has reason to believe that the ball
in play is fractured or imperfect; and to decide those cases in
which the faulty ball is clearly fractured in actually going out of

play and in no way handicaps the player's return, when the point should be scored. In all cases of doubt, however, he should declare a let.

A POINT

Except as provided in Law 6 (9), either player shall lose a point:
   If he fails to make a good service.
   If a good service or a good return having been made by his opponent, he fails to make a good return.
   If he, or his bat, or anything that he wears or carries touches the net or its supports, while the ball is in play.
   If he, or his bat, or anything that he wears or carries, moves the playing surface while the ball is in play.
   If his free hand touches the playing surface while the ball is in play.
   If, before the ball in play shall have passed over the end lines or side lines not yet having touched the playing surface on his side of the table since being struck by his opponent, it comes in contact with him or with anything that he wears or carries.
   If at any time he volleys the ball.

EXPEDITE SYSTEM

If a game be unfinished fifteen minutes after it has begun, the rest of that game and the remaining games of the match shall proceed under the Expedite System. Thereafter, if the service and twelve following strokes of the server are returned by good returns of the receiver, the server shall lose the point. See rules on Service.

A GAME

A game shall be won by the player who first wins 21 points, unless both players shall have scored 20 points, when the winner of the game shall be he who first wins two points more than his opponent.

A MATCH

A match shall consist of one contest for the best of three or best of five games. Play shall be continuous throughout, except that either opposing player is entitled to claim a repose period of not more than five minutes' duration between the third and fourth games of a five-game match.

Note: This rule defines a contest between two players or pairs. A contest consisting of a group of individual matches between two sides is usually distinguished as a 'team match'.

THE CHOICE OF ENDS AND SERVICE

The choice of ends and the right to be server or receiver in every match shall be decided by toss, provided that, if the winner of the toss chooses the right to be server or receiver, the other player shall have the choice of ends, and vice versa, and provided that the winner of the toss, if he prefers it, may require the other player to make the first choice.

THE CHANGE OF ENDS AND SERVICE

Ends: The player who started at one end in a game shall start at the other in the immediately subsequent game and so on, until the end of the match. In the last possible game of the match the players shall change ends when first either player reaches the score 10.

Service: After five points the receiver shall become the server and the server the receiver and so on after each five points until the end of the game or the score 20-all, or until the game be interrupted under the Expedite System. From the score 20-all, or if the game be interrupted under the Expedite System, the service shall change after each point until the end of the game. The player who

74

served first in a game shall be receiver first in the immediately subsequent game, and so on until the end of a match.

OUT OF ORDER OF ENDS OR SERVICE

Ends: If the players have not changed ends when ends should have been changed, the players shall change ends as soon as the mistake is discovered, unless a game has been completed since the error, when the error shall be ignored. In any circumstances all points scored before the discovery shall be reckoned.

Service: If a player serves out of his turn, play shall be interrupted as soon as the mistake is discovered and shall continue with that player serving who, according to the sequence established at the beginning of the match, should be the server at the score that has been reached. In any circumstances all points scored before the discovery shall be reckoned.

DOUBLES

The above Laws shall apply in the Doubles Game except as below:

THE TABLE

The surface of the table shall be divided into two parts by a white line 3 mm ($\frac{1}{8}$ in) broad, running parallel with the side lines and distant equally from each of them. This line shall be termed the centre line.

Note: The doubles centre line may be permanently marked in full length on the table. This is a convenience and in no way invalidates the table for singles play. The part of the table surface on the nearer side of the net and the right of the centre line in respect to the server shall be called the server's right half-court, that on the left in respect to him the server's left half-court. The part of the table surface on the farther side of the net and the left

75

of the centre line in respect to the server shall be called the receiver's right half-court, that on the right in respect to the server
shall be called the receiver's left half-court.

A GOOD SERVICE

The service shall be delivered as otherwise provided in Law 6 (6),
and so that it touches first the server's right half-court or the
centre line on his side of the net and then passing directly over or
around the net, touches the receiver's right half-court or the
centre line on his side of the net.

THE ORDER OF PLAY

The server shall first make a good service, the receiver shall then
make a good return, the partner of the server shall then make a
good return, the partner of the receiver shall then make a good
return, the server shall then make a good return and thereafter
each player alternately in that sequence shall make a good
return.

THE CHOICE OF THE ORDER OF PLAY

The pair who have the right to serve the first five services in any
game shall decide which partner shall do so. In the first game of
the match the opposing pair shall then decide similarly which
shall be the first receiver. In subsequent games the serving pair
shall choose their first server and the first receiver will then be
established automatically to correspond with the first server.

THE ORDER OF SERVICE

Throughout each game, except as provided in the second para-
graph, the first five services shall be delivered by the partner of the
pair who have the right to do so and shall be received by the appropriate partner of the opposing pair. The second five services
shall be delivered by the receiver of the first five services and re-

76

ceived by the partner of the server of the first five services. The third five services shall be delivered by the partner of the server of the first five services and received by the partner of the receiver of the first five services. The fourth five services shall be delivered by the partner of the receiver of the first five services and received by the server of the first five services. The fifth five services shall be delivered as the first five services, and so on, in sequence, until the end of the game or the score 20-all or the introduction of the Expedite System, when the sequence of serving and receiving shall be interrupted, and each player shall serve only one service in turn until the end of the game.

In the last possible game of the match when either pair of players reaches the score 10 the receiving pair must alter the order of serving.

In each game of a match the initial order of receiving shall be opposite to that in the preceding game.

OUT OF ORDER OF RECEIVING

If a player acts as receiver out of his turn play shall be interrupted as soon as the mistake is discovered and shall continue with that player receiving who, according to the sequence established at the beginning or at the score 10 if the sequence has been changed under Law 6 (21), should be receiver at the score which has been reached. In any circumstances all points scored before the discovery shall be reckoned.

CLOTHING

Players shall not wear white or light-coloured clothing which might tend to distract or dazzle the opponent. Any badge or lettering on a playing-garment must not be so large or conspicuous as to break disturbingly its uniform dark colour. The decision as to the offence under this rule shall be with the referee.